Play with Plants

PLAY WITH
PLANTS

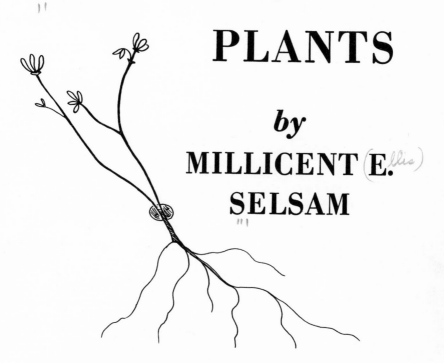

by

MILLICENT (E. *Ellis*)
SELSAM

PICTURES BY JAMES MACDONALD

WILLIAM MORROW AND COMPANY
NEW YORK 1949

Table of Contents

1
Plants Grow From Roots, Stems, Leaves

PLANTS can be fun. In this book you will find many different ways of having fun with plants, and all of them depend on growing things in your home. You can do all the plant experiments described in this book without any garden out of doors.

The most fun you can have with plants comes from making new ones grow. Usually we think of plants as growing from seeds. But there are many other ways of raising them. For instance, you can grow plants from roots, from stems, and even from leaves.

If you want to try to grow a new plant from a root, you must find a root which has a lot of food stored in it. This is because a new plant must have a supply of food when it starts to grow. Sweet potatoes, carrots, beets, turnips, parsnips, and radishes all are roots. They have food stored in them, and that is why they are good to eat. This same food helps a new plant grow.

For instance, you can make a beautiful vine grow out of a sweet potato. Set the sweet potato in a jar of water, so that only the narrow end sits in the water. If you haven't a jar just the right size, stick toothpicks into the potato to support it at the mouth of the jar. Be sure to put the narrow pointed end into the water. Now roots grow from this end. The illustration shows both roots and vine.

Now set the jar in a warm dark place. Keep adding water as it is used up. The new roots will grow out first, and in about ten days you will see the stems starting. As soon as they start, move the sweet potato into a sunlit or brightly lighted window. The whole potato should become covered with stems and purple-veined leaves. You can let the vines trail over the sides of a container set in a hanging bracket or you

NARROW POINTED END
IN WATER
SET IN WARM DARK PLACE

THE SWEET POTATO VINE

NEW ROOTS
GROW OUT FIRST...
STEMS START IN 10 DAYS

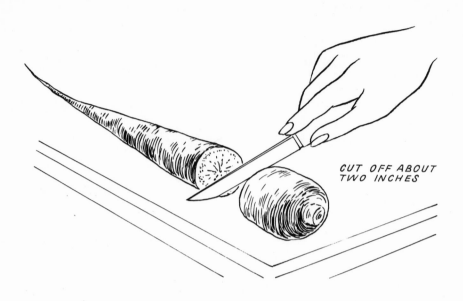

may prefer to tie the stems to cords and let them climb up the window.

When you are choosing a sweet potato, look for one that has some sign of life. If the buds show up as little purple bumps, and if there are some roots still hanging on, you have a good sweet potato to grow. Your vegetable man can help you pick such a one if you explain your purpose to him.

The carrot root is easy to grow, too. First take off the wilted leaves from the top of the carrot. Then cut off 2 inches of the carrot at the big end. Set it in a shallow bowl of water with pebbles or stones around it to hold it in place. If you can't get your own stones, they can be bought at five-and-ten-cent stores.

In a little while, new leaves will grow out of the top. They are thin and feathery, and make a pretty table decoration.

The other roots with stored food—beets, turnips, and parsnips—can be grown in exactly the same way.

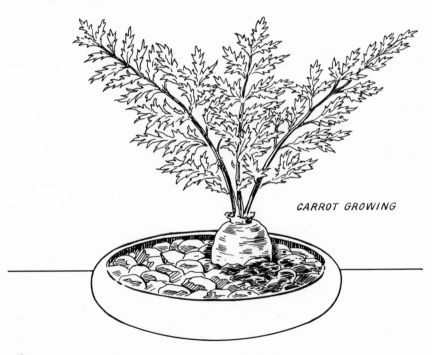

CARROT GROWING

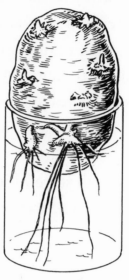

POTATO IN WATER .. ROOTS GROWING AND STEMS STARTING

A plain Irish potato is a stem. It's a funny kind of stem because it grows under the ground. Like the sweet potato, it has food stored in it from which a new plant can grow.

Put the potato in a jar of water, so that only the bottom stays wet. Roots will grow out from the lower end, and new stems and leaves from the eyes or little buds which you can find on every potato. Try cutting off a piece of potato with two or three little buds on

12

it and planting it in a flower pot. Put it about three inches below the surface of the soil. If you water it regularly, a potato plant will grow from this piece. Farmers plant their potato crops by using just such pieces of potato.

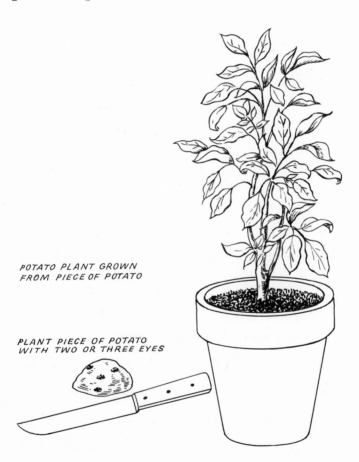

POTATO PLANT GROWN
FROM PIECE OF POTATO

PLANT PIECE OF POTATO
WITH TWO OR THREE EYES

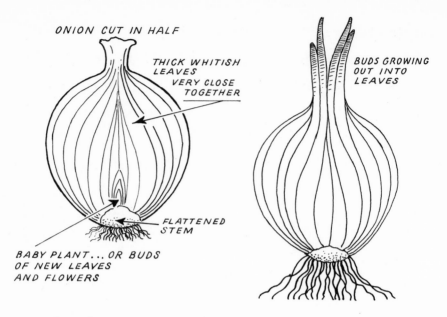

ONION CUT IN HALF

THICK WHITISH
LEAVES
VERY CLOSE
TOGETHER

BUDS GROWING
OUT INTO
LEAVES

FLATTENED
STEM

BABY PLANT...OR BUDS
OF NEW LEAVES
AND FLOWERS

Another stem that has lots of stored food is the onion. An onion doesn't really look like a stem, but that's because it is very much shortened and flattened down, so that all its leaves are close together. We call such a stem a *bulb*. The picture shows what you will find if you cut an onion down through the center.

Onions grow easily. In fact, you often find them growing in the bag without any help at all. If you want to watch an onion grow, set it in a glass of water so that only the bottom will keep wet. New white roots will come out from the bottom of the bulb. The

14

little bud inside then grows into long green leaves. The new young plant uses the food stored in the thick fleshy leaves of the bulb to get started. When your onion tops are about 4 inches high, cut down through the middle of the bulb. You will see that the buds in the center have grown out into leaves.

If you want pretty flowers to grow out of a bulb, try growing the paper-white narcissus. You can buy narcissus bulbs at seed stores and at five-and-tens. You can grow these bulbs in water with pebbles around the bulbs to hold them in place.

First put a layer of pebbles in the bottom of a bowl. Then place the bulbs on them, and add more pebbles until just the ends of the bulbs are sticking out. Add enough water so that it will just touch the bottoms of the bulbs. Keep it at exactly that level. You will have to keep adding a little water each day to keep it there. The bulbs use the water up and it also evaporates in the air.

Place the bowl on a sunny window sill. If you plant the bulbs late in the winter, they will bloom in about three weeks. If you start early in the fall, you

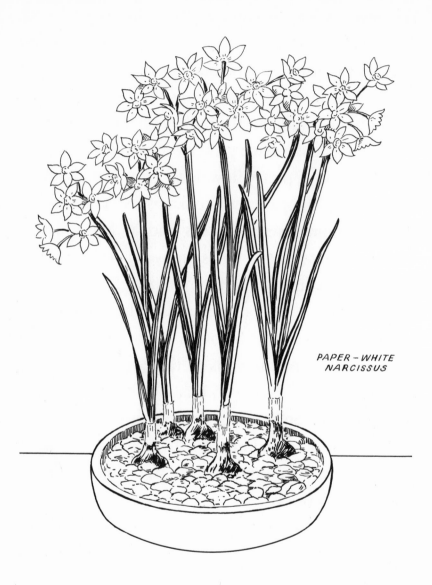

PAPER – WHITE
NARCISSUS

will have to wait longer. The bulbs will take about two months to come into bloom. Narcissus bulbs bloom naturally in the spring. The nearer to this time they are planted in the house, the less time they take to grow.

If you put pussy willow stems into water in early spring, new roots form very quickly near the bottom of the stem. After they have rooted, you can put the pussy willows into soil. You have made a new plant. There are lots of other plants that will root in this way. You can have fun making new plants from old ones.

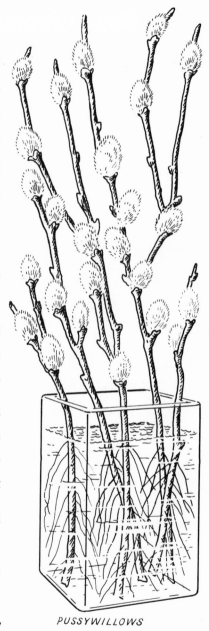

PUSSYWILLOWS

First cut off a piece of stem 3 or 4 inches long. Make your cut just below a place where leaves come out of the stem. Trim off all but two or three leaves. Then plant the piece in moist sand in a small flower pot and set a glass jar over the plant. If you haven't any sand, look for some where there is building going on.

It may take a few weeks before you see that your new plant is growing. Not every single plant you try will root in this way, but lots of plants will. You will have good luck with begonias, geraniums, fuchsias, philodendron, and ivy. When you see new leaves forming, you will know that the piece of stem has made new roots, and so has become a whole new plant. Now is the time to move it into a pot containing soil.

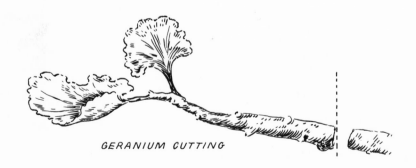

GERANIUM CUTTING

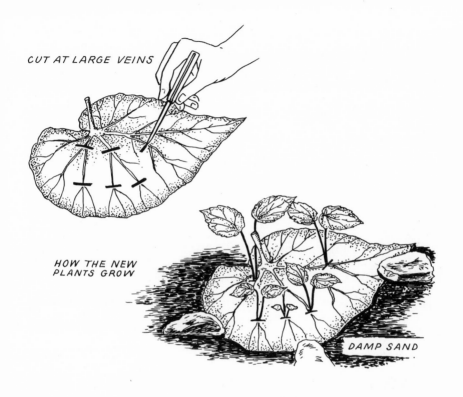

CUT AT LARGE VEINS

HOW THE NEW
PLANTS GROW

DAMP SAND

So far we have started new plants from roots and stems. Starting a new plant from a leaf seems impossible. Yet it can be done with the leaves of some plants.

If you can get hold of a large thick rex begonia leaf, make a cut at each large vein of the leaf, and lay the leaf on damp sand with the under side down. Put pebbles or stones on it to keep it flat.

PUT YOUNG PLANT
INTO POT
CONTAINING SOIL

Now place a glass jar over it to keep it moist, and put it where it will get light. In a few weeks, tiny new plants will form where you made the cuts. When the new little plants are 2 to 3 inches tall, move them into separate small pots containing soil.

You can make lots of new plants from the leaves of the African violet. Take off a leaf with a little piece of the stem attached and stand it up with the stem part buried in the damp sand. Keep it covered with a glass jar. A tiny new plant will grow where the stem hits the sand.

Practically everybody owns a snake plant or knows somebody who does. One of its long leaves can make more than a half-dozen new plants. Here is how

to do it. Cut up the leaf into pieces about 2 inches
long, and put each piece
halfway down into damp
sand. Cover it with glass.
New plants form where
the leaf hits the sand.

If you are interested
in making new plants,

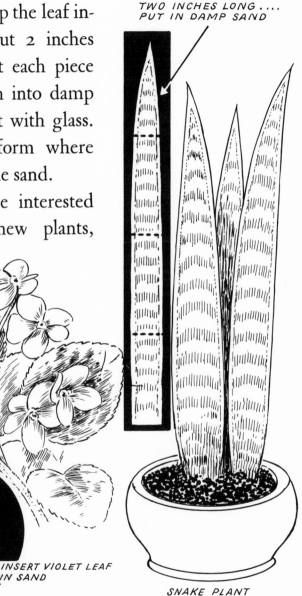

CUT OFF PIECES ABOUT
TWO INCHES LONG....
PUT IN DAMP SAND

AFRICAN
VIOLET

INSERT VIOLET LEAF
IN SAND

SNAKE PLANT

make a simple box for yourself in which to put pieces of stems and leaves to root.

All you need is a shallow wooden box and four panes of glass placed around the four sides of the box with their lower edges resting on the bottom. Moist sand will hold the glass in place. A glass cover will complete the rooting box. You can experiment and find many other plants that will grow from a piece of stem or from a leaf.

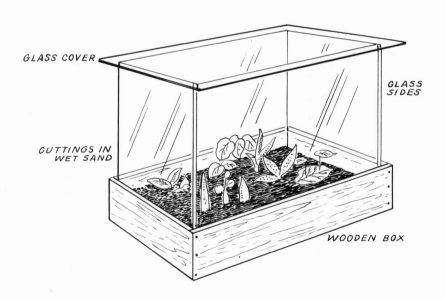

GLASS COVER

GLASS SIDES

CUTTINGS IN WET SAND

WOODEN BOX

2
Plants Grow From Seeds

GETTING new plants to grow from roots, stems, and leaves may have been new to you. Planting seeds to make new plants is something everyone knows about. Instead of buying packages of seeds, use the many seeds you can find among the foods you eat.

You probably know what lentil soup is like. But look closely at a lentil. Although it seems hard and dried up and lifeless, a lentil is a seed and can be made to spring to life.

First soak some lentil seeds overnight. Then line a glass with a paper towel. Wet the paper so that it sticks to the edge of the glass, and keep about an inch of water in the bottom so that the paper will stay

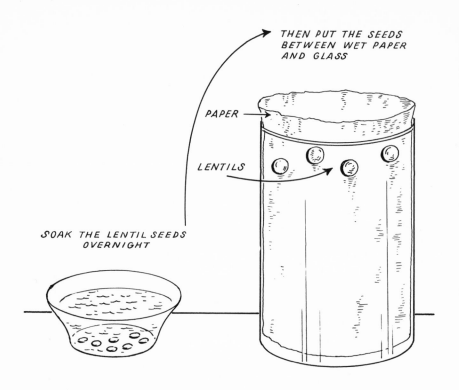

THEN PUT THE SEEDS
BETWEEN WET PAPER
AND GLASS

PAPER →

LENTILS →

SOAK THE LENTIL SEEDS
OVERNIGHT

constantly moist. Lay the seeds between the wet paper and the glass around the top. The picture shows how to do this. In a few days you will see roots growing down and green stems starting up.

This way of growing seeds makes it easy for you to see exactly how the roots and stems grow. However, the plants will die after a few weeks because

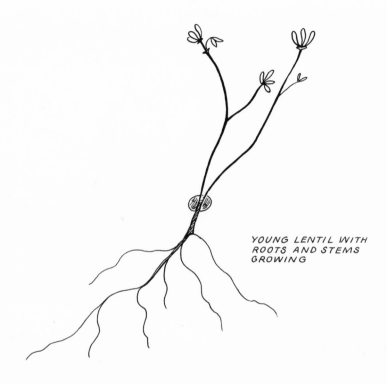

YOUNG LENTIL WITH
ROOTS AND STEMS
GROWING

they can't live for long on water only. If you want them
to grow for a long time, plant the soaked lentil seeds
in small pots containing soil. Cover the seeds with
about ¼ inch of soil, and keep them watered.

The next time you have an orange or grapefruit
or lemon, take the seeds out and save them for planting. Soak the seeds overnight and then plant three or

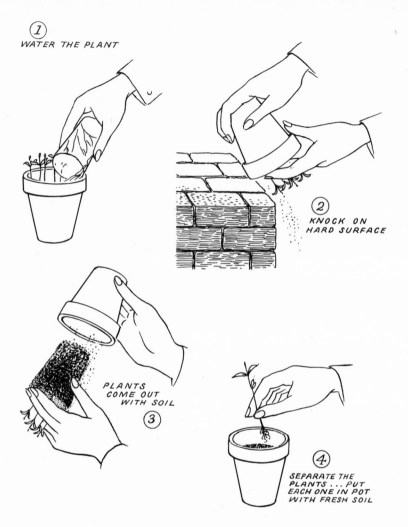

① WATER THE PLANT

② KNOCK ON HARD SURFACE

PLANTS COME OUT WITH SOIL
③

④ SEPARATE THE PLANTS ... PUT EACH ONE IN POT WITH FRESH SOIL

four of them in a small flower pot. Cover them with about ¼ inch of soil. You can start them in plain sand, as well as soil.

GRAPEFRUIT
PLANT

When each of the plants has three or four leaves, you must separate them so that each one has more room to grow in. The best way to do this is to knock out the soil from the pot and the plants with it. Water the soil first. Then hit the edge of the pot against something hard. Turn it upside down and the soil should come out in one piece. It is easy then to separate each plant and put it into a separate small flower pot with fresh soil. When it gets big, you can move it to a bigger pot in the same way.

Grapefruit, lemon, and orange plants have dark green glossy leaves and make pretty house plants.

The picture shows how an alligator pear or avocado plant looks when you grow it. The next time you have an alligator pear salad for dinner, save the big seed in the center of the alligator pear and make a new plant grow from it.

First take the brown papery coat off the seed. Then set it in a jar of water. The top of the jar should hold up the seed so that only the wide, indented bottom part is in the water. Be sure to put this end into the water.

It is best to use a tall jar like an olive jar, for although this seed takes weeks to get started, the roots grow fast and long once they start. Keep it in dim light while only the roots are growing, and then bring it out to the light when the stem starts to grow. You will have to be patient. It will take a long time, but you will be excited when you see the big seed split at the top to let out the stem and leaves of the new alligator pear plant. The stems grow tall and have large leaves. After the plant has been in the water about two months, add soil gradually till it has replaced all the water, or else plant it in a big pot.

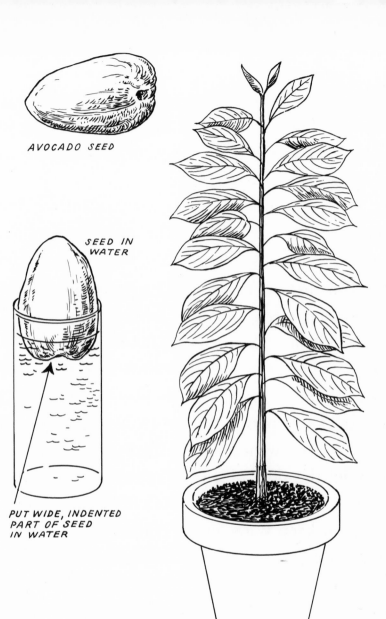

AVOCADO SEED

SEED IN
WATER

PUT WIDE, INDENTED
PART OF SEED
IN WATER

AVOCADO PLANT

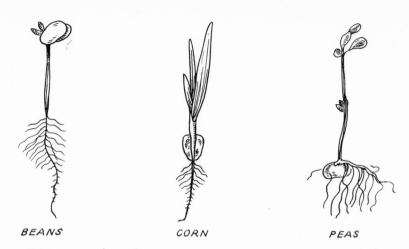

BEANS   CORN   PEAS

You can plant beans, peas, corn, cantaloupe seeds, watermelon seeds, and other seeds that you can find in your kitchen. Canary seed is fun to plant, too.

If you want to keep the plants from these seeds growing for a long time, then plant them in soil in regular flower pots.

If you just want to see *how* they grow, plant them between the sides of a glass and wet paper—just as you did for the lentil seeds. Soak the seeds overnight first, and keep water in the bottom of the glass to keep the paper wet. Watch roots, stems, and leaves come out of the seed. Each plant has a different way of growing. A pea doesn't grow in the same way as a bean. There is only one good way of finding out how a plant grows. Watch it, and make little pictures of what you see, so that you can compare it with the way other seeds grow.

You won't find grass seed in the kitchen, but if you can get hold of some you can have fun with it.

If you sprinkle grass seed over a wet bath sponge or sponge powder puffs, you can turn them into little mounds of grass. The sponge must be soaked first, and then set in a saucer with water in it. Be sure the water in the saucer never dries up, for the grass seed must be kept constantly damp. After the seed is sprinkled over the sponge, cover it with a glass dish and set it in a sunny window. When you see tiny young blades of grass, you can take the glass cover off.

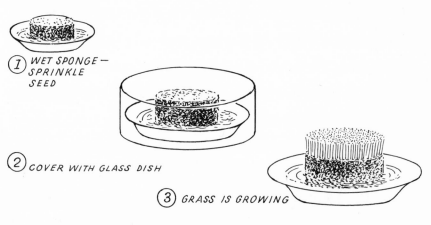

1) WET SPONGE — SPRINKLE SEED

2) COVER WITH GLASS DISH

3) GRASS IS GROWING

3
How Seeds Grow

WHEN you tried planting grapefruit or orange or cantaloupe seeds, you took them out of what we call a fruit. Scientifically speaking, a fruit is the part of a plant that has seeds in it. Since this is so, there are a lot of things we call vegetables that are really fruits. It is hard to think of a green pea pod or a string bean as a fruit. But they have seeds in them and so a scientist would call them fruit. The same thing is true of a tomato, a cucumber, and a squash. Anyone can find the seeds in all these.

When you crack the outside of a walnut or a peanut, you are cracking the wall of the fruit. The seed is inside. There are many other fruits among the dif-

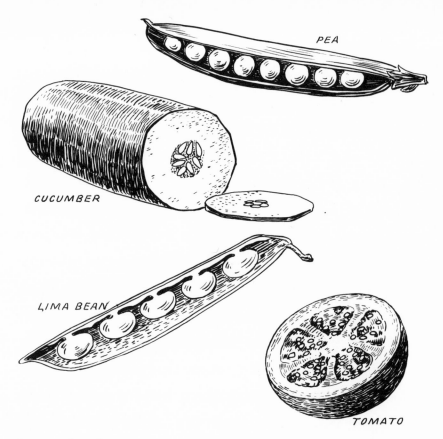

PEA

CUCUMBER

LIMA BEAN

TOMATO

ferent foods you eat. See how many others you can find.

Seeds are wonderful things. They look dry and dead, but if you give them water and warmth they will come to life. This happens because inside every seed there are the beginnings of a new plant. Let's look into a seed and find out.

We'll choose a big one to work on, so that the parts will be easy to see. Soak some lima bean seeds overnight so that they will swell and be full of water. Look for the scar on the side of the bean. The scar shows where the seed was attached to the inside of the bean pod. Now take off the seed coats. They should slip off easily when the seed is wet. The picture shows how the bean looks now. What you have left can be split into two parts. Do this carefully and gently. These two parts are called seed leaves. They have lots of food stored in them. Attached to them you can see a very tiny baby plant.

Look at this baby plant carefully. Use a magnifying glass if you can. Root, stem, and leaves will grow out from this baby plant.

The mystery of the seed is solved. Inside a seed we have found a baby plant and some food to start off its life. All it needs is water, warmth, and air in order to grow. The tiny baby plant inside a seed can become a big plant. A new young plant cannot grow without using the food stored in the seed leaves of the seed. Proving this is an interesting experiment.

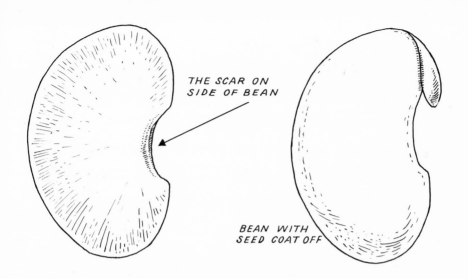

THE SCAR ON
SIDE OF BEAN

BEAN WITH
SEED COAT OFF

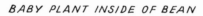

BABY PLANT INSIDE OF BEAN

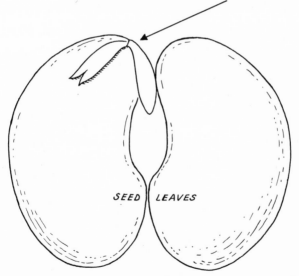

SEED LEAVES

BEAN SPLIT IN TWO (GREATLY MAGNIFIED)

Soak three dried lima bean seeds overnight. Line a glass with wet paper towel, and keep water in the bottom of the glass. Now place one whole seed between the paper and the glass.

Carefully remove one of the seed leaves from the second bean seed without injuring the baby plant. Then place it between the paper and the glass.

Cut the seed leaves of the third bean seed so that only half of one seed leaf will remain with the baby plant. Place it, too, between the glass and the paper.

Now you have three bean seeds ready to grow.

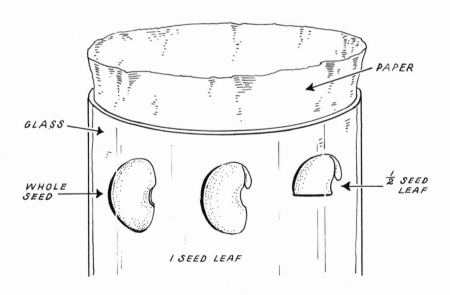

The first has both seed leaves. The second has only one seed leaf. The third has half of one seed leaf.

Watch them grow. You will soon see that the biggest plant grows from the first bean seed. Of course the reason is that this baby plant has the most food. By the time all the food in the seed leaves is used up by the growing plant, it has leaves of its own which can make new food for it.

Starch is one of the foods in the seed leaves. It can also be found in many of the foods we eat. It makes up most of the food in potatoes and rice, for example. You can try this simple way of testing for starch. Make a weak iodine solution by putting a medicine dropperful of iodine into half a glass of water. Drop the iodine solution with a dropper onto a slice of bread or a few grains of rice or a slice of potato. If the food you are testing turns dark blue, you have proved that starch is present.

Now try the iodine solution on a thin slice of *soaked* bean seed. Then you can see the proof of the statement that beans have starch in their seed leaves.

We wait till the ground has warmed up to plant

most seeds for a very good reason. Seeds need warmth in order to grow. Try this experiment to prove it.

Soak 30 radish seeds overnight. Lay 15 of them down on wet paper towel in a dish. Cover them and put the dish into the refrigerator.

Do the same thing with the other 15 seeds, but keep the dish at room temperature instead of putting it into the refrigerator.

After two days, count the number of growing seeds in each dish, and keep a record of how many growing ones were in the refrigerator and how many in the dish that was kept at room temperature.

You will have proof then that seeds need warmth to grow.

Besides water and warmth, seeds need air in order to start growth. Here is another experiment to test this statement. Collect three small glass jars of the same size. Baby-food jars or any other small jars will do. Fill one jar with water from the faucet. This water has air dissolved in it. Add 15 radish seeds.

Fill the second jar with water boiled, to drive out all the air and then cooled. Add 15 radish seeds.

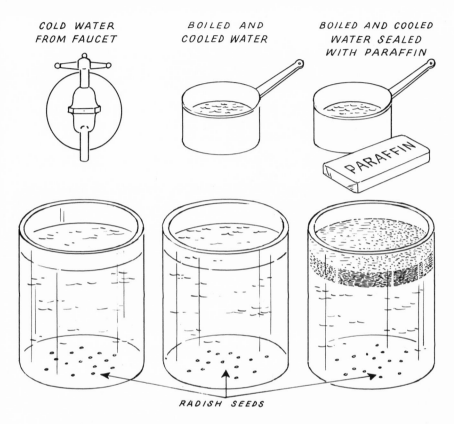

COLD WATER
FROM FAUCET

BOILED AND
COOLED WATER

BOILED AND COOLED
WATER SEALED
WITH PARAFFIN

PARAFFIN

RADISH SEEDS

Fill the third jar with boiled and cooled water. Add 15 radish seeds. Seal this jar by pouring melted paraffin over the surface of the water. All three jars contain the same number of seeds—15 in each one. After two days, count the number of seeds in each jar that have started to grow. Keep a careful record of the results of your experiment.

4
About Experiments

BEFORE we go on with more experiments and things to do with plants, it is important to understand what an experiment is. In an experiment you make things happen to prove something. Let's take as an example the experiment in which you proved that seeds need air in order to grow. It seems easy just to put some seeds in tap water that contains air and watch to see if the seeds will start to grow. But this in itself isn't enough. You haven't proved anything until you try to grow seeds in water that has *no air* in it. In order to prove that seeds need air to grow, you have to compare what happens to seeds in water containing air with the results you get when seeds are put in water that is without air.

It is the same with every other experiment you try. If you want to prove that seeds need warmth to grow, you grow some seeds in a warm place and compare them with another set in a cold place. After you finish this book, you may want to make up some experiments of your own. Remember that no matter what you want to prove, you should make one part of the experiment where something is present, and another part where that something is absent.

In doing the last few experiments, you have probably already learned the next rule about all experiments. When you set up an experiment, you imagine you will remember forever just when you set it up and exactly what you did. In a few days, though, you find yourself wishing you had put labels on the jars or whatever else you were using.

So from now on, be sure that you label things carefully and put down the dates and figures. Scientists who do experiments all the time write things down, and keep careful notes of their results.

The more experiments you do, the sooner you will find out that an experiment does not always turn out exactly the way you think it should. Don't be disappointed. Try to find out why it didn't work the way you thought it should. Sometimes important discoveries are made when experiments do not turn out the way they were expected to. You can have lots of fun with experiments that turn out right. But you can have even more fun trying to find out why experiments go wrong.

LABEL YOUR EXPERIMENTS

5
Plants Need Water

IF YOU ever watered a plant in a pot, you probably
know why flower pots have holes in the bottom. If
there is too much water in the pot, the extra water can
run out of the hole. Some plants are grown in jars or
dishes without holes, but in these cases pebbles or
stones are put at the bottom under the soil so that
extra water can run into them. It is important to have
ways of getting rid of extra water in flower pots or
containers, because too much water can kill the plants.

If you have any plants to take care of, here is the
way to water them. Wait until the surface of the soil
feels dry before you water. When you do water a plant,
do it thoroughly. Be sure the soil is thoroughly soaked

by adding water until the extra water comes out of the bottom of the pot.

After you have watered plants a few times, you will probably begin to wonder how the water gets into the plant from the soil. The part of the plant that is underground is the root, so somehow the water must get into the root.

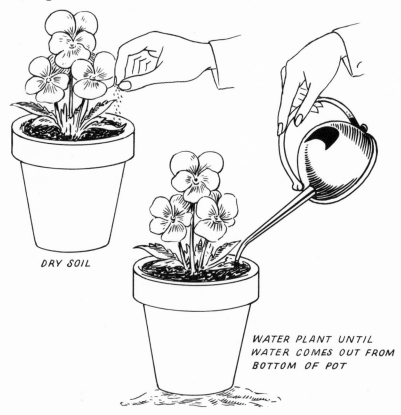

DRY SOIL

WATER PLANT UNTIL
WATER COMES OUT FROM
BOTTOM OF POT

LEAF

STEM

ROOT HAIRS

YOUNG RADISH PLANT SHOWING ROOT HAIRS

If you used radish seeds in the experiments on seeds needing air and warmth, you must have noticed that young radish roots look practically like little bottle brushes. This is due to the many little root hairs that come out from the main root. Water passes from the soil into these root hairs, which are very fine and thin-walled.

In order to get a good look at radish root hairs, try this experiment.

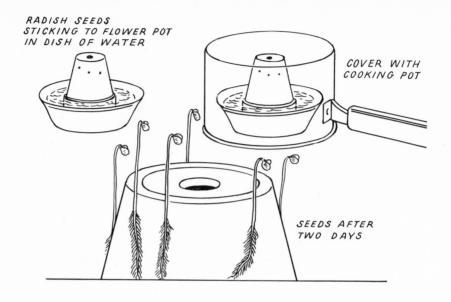

RADISH SEEDS
STICKING TO FLOWER POT
IN DISH OF WATER

COVER WITH
COOKING POT

SEEDS AFTER
TWO DAYS

Soak a clean small flower pot in water for an hour. Then place it upside down in water. Stick *soaked* radish seeds onto the outside of the wet flower pot. It's tricky, but with a little practice you can get the radish seeds to stay on. Now cover the whole thing with a cooking pot to keep the flower pot moist and dark. Roots grow better in the dark. The illustration shows the way the radish seeds will look when you start them and after two days.

The water that gets into the root through the root hairs travels up through the root into the stem.

46

Since a carrot is a root, a big one, let's see how it is suited to its job of carrying water up to the stem.

First cut the carrot straight down through the middle. You can see that the carrot has a central core. In this center are tubes which carry water up from the soil to the stem. If you cut a thin slice across the carrot and hold it up to the light, you will see this central core clearly.

Now prove to yourself that the carrot supplies water to its stems and leaves. Get a young carrot with fresh stems and leaves and freshen them up still more

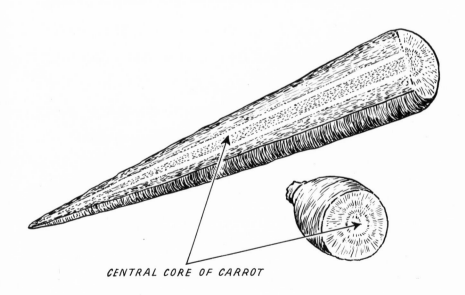

CENTRAL CORE OF CARROT

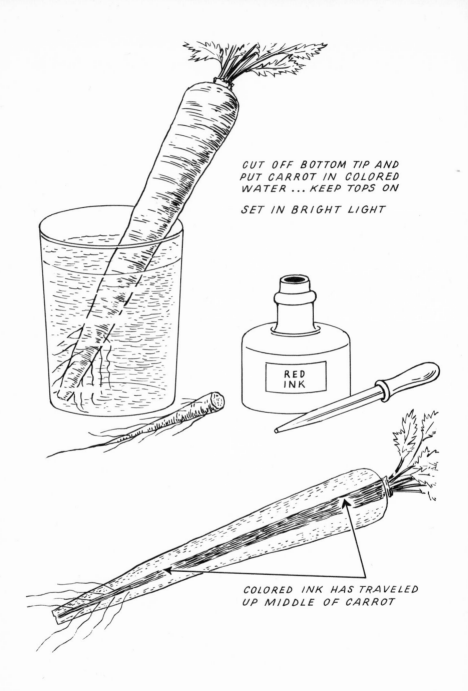

CUT OFF BOTTOM TIP AND
PUT CARROT IN COLORED
WATER ... KEEP TOPS ON

SET IN BRIGHT LIGHT

RED
INK

COLORED INK HAS TRAVELED
UP MIDDLE OF CARROT

by cutting off the bottom tip of the root and putting the carrot in a glass of water.

Meanwhile, color some water with green or red ink. Use two droppersful of ink to a half glass of water.

Now put the freshened-up carrot into the colored water and set it in a bright light for several hours. Cut down through the middle of the carrot, and notice where the colored ink is.

From the root of the plant, water travels up through the stem into the leaves. You can watch this happen in a stalk (stem) of celery. Freshen up a stalk of celery by cutting off the bottom half inch and setting the stalk in water for about an hour. Then put the stalk of celery in water colored by red ink, just as you did for the carrot. Set it in bright light.

In about an hour, look to see if the leaves of the celery have turned reddish. When they have, you can take the celery out and examine it. First cut off a piece about an inch from the bottom. The illustration on the next page shows where you will find the red ink.

Now take the rest of the stalk, and with a small

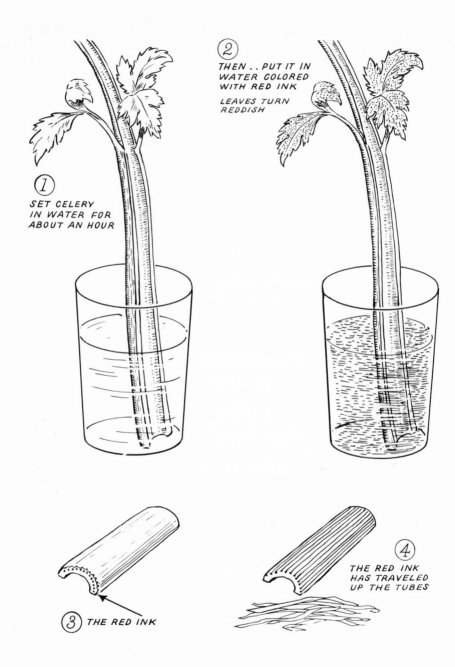

① SET CELERY IN WATER FOR ABOUT AN HOUR

② THEN .. PUT IT IN WATER COLORED WITH RED INK

LEAVES TURN REDDISH

③ THE RED INK

④ THE RED INK HAS TRAVELED UP THE TUBES

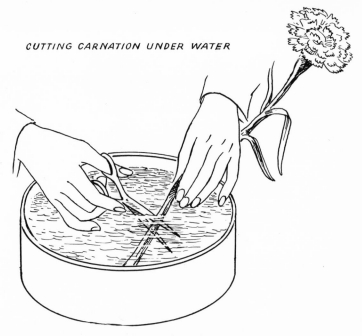

knife scrape off the outer layers of stalk until you come to red lines. These red lines are tubes that carry water up through the stem.

You probably have seen green carnations on St. Patrick's Day. These carnations were colored green in the same way that the leaves of the celery were colored red. You can color a white carnation yourself. First cut off the end of the stem under water. This prevents air from blocking the tubes through which the water passes up the stem. Then place the carnation in water colored with red, green, or purple ink,

51

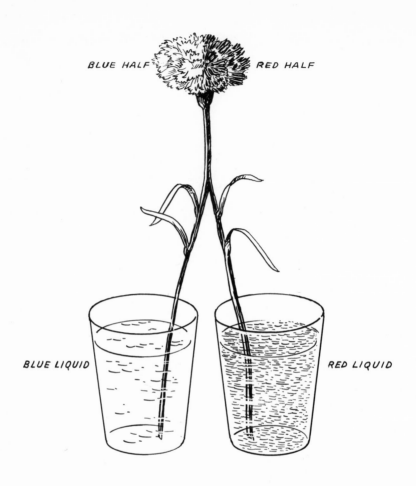

BLUE HALF   RED HALF

BLUE LIQUID   RED LIQUID

and put it in bright light for a few hours. The petals will become reddish, greenish, or purplish, depending on what color ink you used.

If you want to have fun, try splitting the stem of a carnation into two parts without tearing them from the flower. Put each part into a differently colored liquid. Keep the flower in bright light for a few hours. The petals will become colored with the color of the liquid that reaches them, and you will have a carnation part of which is one color and part another.

If water is constantly passing from the ground into the roots of a plant and up to the stem and leaves

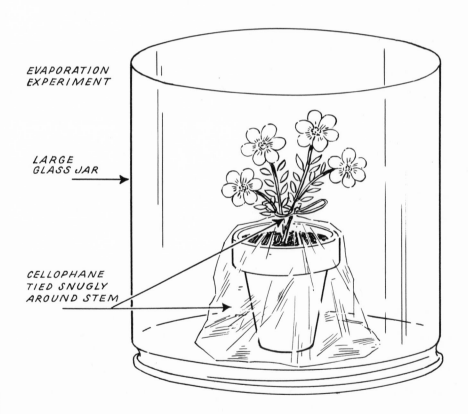

EVAPORATION
EXPERIMENT

LARGE
GLASS JAR

CELLOPHANE
TIED SNUGLY
AROUND STEM

and flowers, it must leave the plant somehow. It does this by evaporating from the surface of the leaves.

You can see for yourself that water leaves the plant. Take a plant growing in a small flower pot and water it well. Wrap cellophane or wax paper around the pot and tie it snugly around the stem of the plant. This will keep water from the pot and soil inside the paper. Now set a large glass jar or vase over the pot. Put it in a bright light. If water evaporates from the leaves, it will collect on the glass.

6
Plants Need Light

WHAT a plant looks like depends very much on how much light it gets. Try growing the same kind of plant in very bright light, in dim light, and in the dark. You will be amazed at how different it can look.

Grow some soaked radish, bean, pea, or lentil seeds in glass containers lined with wet paper such as you used before in growing lentils. Prepare three containers with about six seeds in each. Keep water in the bottom of the containers.

Put one container in very bright light (sunlight if possible), one in dim light (far from a window), and one in the dark (covered with a pot or in a dark closet).

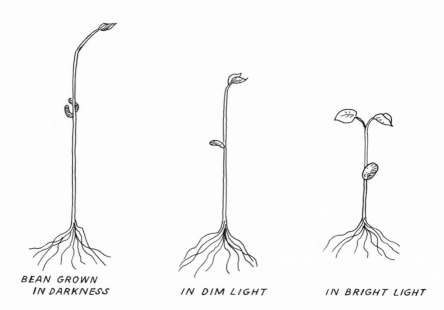

BEAN GROWN
IN DARKNESS   IN DIM LIGHT   IN BRIGHT LIGHT

Remember to see that there is water in the bottom of the jars. After five days, compare the looks of your plants. The picture shows bean plants that have grown in the dark, in dim light, and in bright light.

Have you ever seen a lopsided plant with the leaves all turned in one direction? It is easy to change a lopsided plant into a straight one. All you have to do is to turn the plant around so that the other side will get light.

Leaves and young stems always bend toward the light. If you keep plants on your window sill, keep

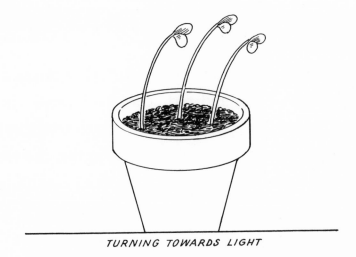

turning them around so that all sides will get light. Then they will be nicely shaped.

If you want to see plants really bend over far toward the light, grow some bean or pea, lentil or radish seeds in small flower pots in the dark until they are about an inch high. Then place the pots on a brightly lighted window sill and notice how soon the stems will bend toward the light.

Sunlight is made up of lots of colors. If you have ever seen a rainbow, you have seen these colors.

In the last experiment, we showed how plants

bend toward light. Now we can do another experiment to show which of the colors in sunlight the plants bend to most.

Get three small flower pots, three shoe boxes, and some yellow, blue, and red cellophane. Soak about 60 canary seeds and plant 20 seeds in each small flower pot. Cover all three with a large pot so that the seeds will grow in the dark until they are about 1 inch high.

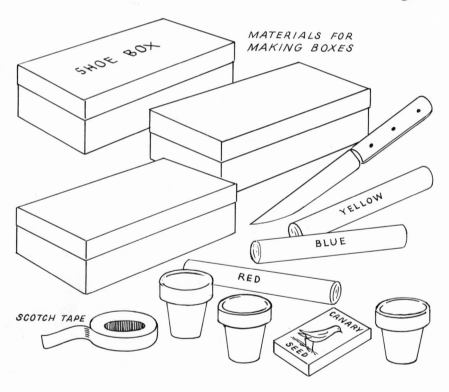

MATERIALS FOR MAKING BOXES

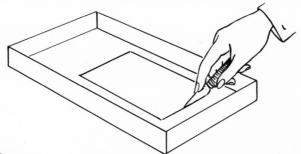

① CUT WINDOW IN TOP OF SHOE BOX

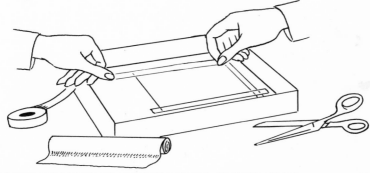

② FASTEN CELLOPHANE WINDOW WITH SCOTCH TAPE
ON INSIDE OF SHOE BOX COVER

③ PLACE POT INSIDE OF SHOE BOX

④ PUT COVER WITH CELLOPHANE ON BOX

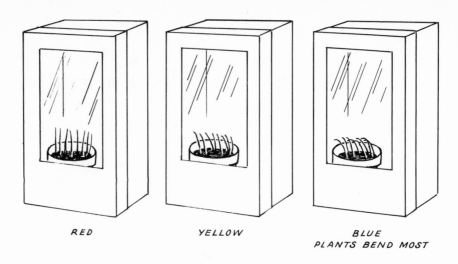

RED   YELLOW   BLUE
PLANTS BEND MOST

Now cut a window in each shoe box, and cover one window with red cellophane, the second with blue, and the third with yellow. Use Scotch tape to keep the cellophane in place. Put one flower pot in each box, and put the cover of the shoe box on. Put all three boxes containing the pots in bright light but not in direct sunlight. Keep the plants watered, and look at them after five hours and again after one day. You will find that the plants in the box with the blue cellophane bend the most.

Stems usually grow straight up. Even if you lay a plant on its side, the stem will turn and grow upwards. You can make a plant bend into funny shapes by doing this experiment. Put 10 soaked radish seeds in a glass jar lined with wet paper. Grow them in the dark until the stems are about 1 inch long. Now pour off the extra water from the bottom of the glass jar and turn the jar on its side. Keep it in the dark. The picture shows the way the plants should look in about 24 hours.

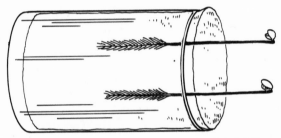

POUR OFF WATER ... PUT JAR ON SIDE
KEEP IT IN THE DARK

PLANTS IN 24 HOURS

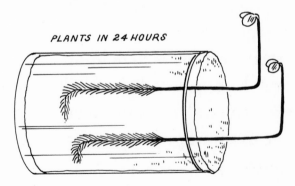

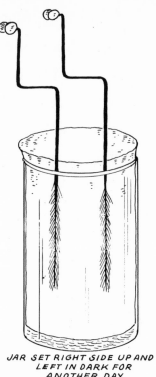

JAR SET RIGHT SIDE UP AND
LEFT IN DARK FOR
ANOTHER DAY

Now turn the jar right side up. Put some water in again and leave it for another day in the dark. The stems will grow straight up again, and your plants will look as they do in the illustration.

You will notice that roots always grow down and stems always grow up no matter in what position the plant is put.

Don't stop experimenting with plants just because this book is ending. It should be only the beginning of your discoveries of what plants are like. If you read more about them, you will find more to learn and many more interesting ways in which you can play with plants.